AF269008

INTO THE INNER LIFE

Into the Inner Life

Carroll Blair

Aveon Publishing Company

ISBN: 978-1-936430-38-3

Library of Congress Control Number
2011904326

Aveon Publishing Co.
P.O. Box 380739
Cambridge, MA 02238-0739 USA

Also by Carroll Blair

Grains of Thought
Facing the Circle
Reel to Real
Shifting Tides
Reaches
Out of Silence
Quarter Notes
By Rays of Light
Gnosis of the Heart
Soul Reflections
Beneath and Beyond the Surface
Of Courage and Commitment
For Today and Tomorrow
In Meditation
Sightings Along the Journey
Through Desert's Fire
Offerings to Pilgrims
Human Natures
(Of Animal and Spiritual)
Atoms from the Suns of Solitude
Colors of Devotion
Voicings
Through the Shadows
As the World Winds Flow

You have a treasure deep within you, a treasure
worth more than all worldly wealth you see
before you, but you will have to work hard to
get to it . . . what will you do? Will you engage the
work, making your way to a life transcendent,
or will you live and die on the surface of your life,
never knowing the great treasure of your life . . .

INTO THE INNER LIFE

If you are not living your music you are not harmonizing with the music of life, of the universe, of the soul.

Where you are most aware, most alert, most creative . . . there is your deepest reality.

One lives to the degree that one is
spiritually awake.

The way to self is the way to all, yet
in the most humble of ways, in the
most selfless of journeys.

You are born with the means to find your way to the spiritual of your life.

If you always feel that you don't know enough or haven't experienced enough to begin *your* journey, you will never begin.

All forms of self-discipline lead to self-realization, and on to enlightenment.

The passion to find one's way is part of the way.

As the body gains strength in the course of a long physical journey, so the spirit gains strength as one continues on one's spiritual journey.

The inner life is created in the odyssey to one's inner treasure.

When not going further, going deeper into the
spiritual dimension of one's life, where is one
going . . .

The measure of inner depth that may be
created is great, but there is a price to pay
for every clearing, for every deepening of
inner being that takes place.

INTO THE INNER LIFE

Is it not in the realm of space where one is able to move about freely? And does not matter block one's way, restricting movement, and when carried, *weighing one down*? . . . And is it not in the world of mind and spirit where one can truly be free, the bondage to the material world keeping many from that freedom?

Your wealth is inside you, but you must still go to it — must go to *you*.

The world is not for you to do with what you please, but neither are you for the world to do with what it pleases.

The material world is a carnival of the fleeting.

Manifests of the temporal continue on and on forever coming into being, but they are still of the temporal.

How many pursue what is false when they can have what is true.

Many do not realize their spiritual birthright,
and die as vagrants who've been left a large
inheritance of which they never knew.

How much weight is lifted from one's
life, how much freedom follows and time
that is no longer wasted when one frees
oneself from the clutches of false hopes
and pursuits.

Would one not be considered a fool who would
put the furnace on in his house and then open
all the windows? Yet this is what many do
regarding the passion and energy of their lives,
casting them to the random winds of the outer
world rather than using them to fuel the domain
of their inner world — their spiritual world,
where all good things emanate and mature,
to then be given to the world.

The life of everyone speaks in hints telling
him, telling her what they should be doing
and which direction they should be going.

One's compass is always off, one's course always wrong when not travelling on one's own path.

To discover the essence of one's existence . . . this is the goal of the purposeful life; the goal that allows all goals of a profound nature to be realized.

Subjectively speaking no two people are
born into the same world.

You are a part of all, yet also apart from all.

Do you see that no one has seen what you
have seen, heard what you have heard, has
felt what you have felt, touched what you
have touched . . . not in the way you have
seen it, heard it, felt it, touched it.

What are you if not a world unto yourself
with forces and potentials of a world ever
coming into being?

If you look only to the teachings of others
you will never find *your* truth, *your* wisdom . . .
might you not also have something to share,
to give, to teach?

It is easier to walk only where others have
walked before you, but is that what you
want? Is it all that you want? . . . Is it?

When going to *something* there are always things to forever walk away from. Are you prepared to walk away . . .

One doesn't grow spiritually, mentally, emotionally without a strong sense or feeling that one needs to grow.

Not all particulars of self-discovery are joyous,
but they are all rich in potential for higher
growth that can lead to the greatest of joy.

Profound transformation does not happen in a
moment, but what can, is the awakening that
a transformation must begin.

How extraordinary a mind *can* be, a heart *can* be, a spirit *can* be, but not automatically.

The true battle to be fought and treasure to be won is not outside one, but within one.

Like going from a darkened room into one of
light . . . going from one's animal nature to one's
spiritual — but not as easily . . . (surely not as
easily).

To realize one's higher self one must travel
deeply into oneself.

The journey must begin before the path is
discovered.

When one discovers one's path everything
foreign to it is immediately recognized and
everything harmonious embraced.

Many agonize because they can't find their way,
but continue to allow others to get in the way
of finding it.

The time devoted to "staking one's claim in
the world" takes from the time of making one's
way to the eternal.

The total involvement with everyday living
is a kind of suicide, for it (like suicide) is
also a form of escape.

Like the body, the spiritual dimension of a life
gets the nourishment it needs, or dies.

You have the power within you to raise the dead to life . . . in this life . . . in your life.

To not save part of the day for the spiritual of oneself is to lose the whole day to the temporal of oneself.

Time itself is priceless, but one's time can never be worth more than the value of that to which it is given.

Many wish their lives to be richer, fuller, but refuse to free themselves from the clutter in their lives that bars the way to fulfillment.

Adding to one's life has much to do with the elimination of the trivial.

Every day in the human world loss of life takes place without physical demise.

How many have searched solely outside
themselves for the time of their lives as their
lives' time slipped away . . .

To constantly reach out to the allure of
the fleeting is to move further away
from the treasure within.

Some people spend their lives trying to decipher
what is real; others live their illusions never
pondering the question of reality.

The part of human-being that is the greatest
obstacle to enlightenment is the part that
doesn't want to let go.

What a difference there is between "grabbing" all the life you can and *absorbing* all the life you can.

Reflect on how much of what you possess can be taken away by the world . . . only what is left can you truly claim to be yours.

Profound happiness cannot be attained without fulfillment, and fulfillment cannot be attained without the cultivation of an inner life.

What is not realized spiritually inside oneself will never be found by one outside oneself.

Man could travel to the ends of the universe and not reap the benefit that would be received from a journey inward to the very depths of his being.

Like homeless exiles wandering the earth . . . they who never make the journey to themselves.

Be one surrounded by worldly wealth,
without inner treasure one is lost.

Very little is more than enough for the one
whose inner world holds much.

42

Even in darkness one can see light if one's soul
is full of light.

No one can stand upright with a slew of petty
wants and ambitions clinging to his life.

43

The compromised soul can never be whole.

How can one appreciate the majesty of Life,
the grandness of its wonder and beauty if
mainly preoccupied with the smallness of
the temporal that permeates the everyday
world?

One cannot wake to the paradise outside oneself
before waking to a paradise within.

Before one is man, before one is woman,
one is spirit.

As there is fruitless action, so is there fruitful idleness.

Sometimes the best thing to do for the health of a spirit is nothing . . . the prelude to a spiritual spring.

The call to enlightenment is not done with a shout, but a whisper.

The crowd is too noisy to hear, too restless to perceive the subtle and refined.

47

Silence has room for everything, noise,
for nothing but itself.

It is by going inside that one learns best
how to live outside.

If you are not in touch with yourself can you
really be in touch with anything else . . .

How can one respond truthfully, substantively
to what is outside him if he doesn't listen
carefully to what is inside him . . .

All are solitary in their birth and in their death, yet many spend their lives fleeing from solitude.

Sometimes the time of one's life isn't a frolic from one party to another, but a time of quiet reflection.

Nothing goes hand in hand like silence and
solitude . . . (and no hands are there more
powerful or beautiful).

Everyone can go where no one has gone
before — in himself . . . in herself.

The inner world too is filled with mirrors reflecting from all angles the makeup of its nature, often changing for those who continue to create depth and expand the scope of their lives.

What you do in your life . . . does it draw you closer to or further away from that part of you which is one with the eternal?

The spiritual sustenance that nourishes one most cannot be brought to one by anyone else; it must be acquired or discovered by oneself.

The entire history of the world cannot teach you more about your life than your own experiences can teach you.

Though perhaps shared in part with others,
the true journey of one's life cannot be
known to another.

All pay a price for their lives, and no two
prices are the same.

INTO THE INNER LIFE

It is a great advantage to know one's path at
an early age, and also its cost . . . to know
what must be done in labor and sacrifice
to achieve the goals of one's life.

All higher growth is seeded in the honest
examination of oneself.

The distance most trivial between people is
that of the physical.

The more individuality one possesses the
closer one is to the essence of All.

56

Self-discovery is a process of both discovery and self-creation.

One needs time to oneself to discover what kind of self exists, and could exist.

The creation of self (of higher self) is a spiritual work of art.

One must eventually forget everything one's been told about what life is or what it's supposed to be, and peer out into the world with one's own eyes and reflect deeply upon what one sees if one is to ever know the power of individual thought, of individual being.

Life does not exist to be questioned, but a human being cannot be fully human, cannot realize the better part of himself or herself without the questioning.

It is not sufficient to have enough mind to embrace truth; one also has to have enough heart.

INTO THE INNER LIFE

It is a blessing that not all things in life are
resolved, leaving the door open for new
insights that lead to further insight that
leads to further growth, creating greater
understanding and the capacity to live
with more passion and compassion,
intensity and love.

To perceive the beauty of life's simplicities
requires an openness to its complexities.

Everything that enters your life serves its purpose in helping you to create yours — (i.e., if you allow it to).

If you are suffering pains that others aren't suffering you are being offered insight and truth that others aren't being offered.

It takes courage to live one's life . . . to
live *your* life.

One cannot love without courage; one
cannot be courageous without love.

Love is the sunlight that raises the harvests
of the soul, but it is also the rain.

What birth of the flesh is without pain?
And what spiritual birth, being so much
greater, bringing new light and creation
into being, could ever be free of pain?

INTO THE INNER LIFE

To flee from spiritual suffering is to flee from the greatest gift that life will ever give to you.

The most brave or cowardly moment anyone can experience in life is known to those who, through revelation or epiphany realize with full clarity the price that must be met to free oneself from the dominance of one's animal nature, to move from the base and superficial into the spiritual and profound, that is, to become what a human being is capable of becoming, and thus proceed with this realization to either begin or turn away from beginning the arduous journey to fulfilling the promise of human spiritualization.

What is more important: discovering your
path, and taking it — discovering your work,
and doing it — growing into the most mature
and spiritualized being that you are capable of
becoming, and embracing it — or doing and
being what others want you to do and be,
forfeiting the actualization of your best
to please the selfishness of others . . .

And would it not be selfishness on your part
to give in to the selfish demands of others
regarding your life, to turn away from your
inner power that, once developed, could be
used to give true benefit to others?

All that life or the world can really use from anyone that is to its benefit is what is inside one, what grows from within.

One who spends his life trying to "fit in" will never bring anything to life that is quite his own, that quite "fits."

What can the measure of one be worth if not
as seed living and bringing forth from the soil
of oneself . . .

How can one *be there* for anyone else if one
is never there for himself . . . in himself . . .

Only the rich in spirit know how to live
inside their hearts.

Anything that prevents one or hinders
one from developing the higher nature
is a corrupting force.

All may go on in their lives, but not everyone goes forward.

Some live their lives as if they were passengers on a train or bus, leaving the driving to someone else.

INTO THE INNER LIFE

You have everything inside you that
is necessary to be what you can be . . .
does the peach tree need to know of
the apple or orange trees to bear its
fruit? Or need the strawberry bush
have permission from the blueberry
to be what it was meant to be?

If you want a deeper, richer, more
meaningful experience of life, the place
to look must always be inside yourself.

Are you more interested in polishing and
decorating your surface, or creating depth
beneath the surface . . .

There's no doubt that throughout humankind
there has been spiritual seed never sown,
waiting to bring forth treasure the world
has never known. A tragedy beyond
measure that such wealth (such treasure)
has gone to waste, depriving humankind
of what it needs most.

Reflect on the depths of the ocean and how
much life is there . . . consider the potential
depths of inner being — how much life
may be present as yet unknown, waiting
to be realized.

"Steady as she goes" is a sentiment wise to
hold in one's mind when descending deep
into the soul.

To lose touch with silence is to lose touch
with the sacred, with the eternal, for silence
is the portal that leads to all pathways to the
sacred, to the eternal.

All are children of the invisible.

To embrace the temporal as the center of your
life is to embrace a world of fantasy.

Though you are not forever, you are part of
Forever, with an invitation to partake in the
powerful force of that which always is and
will always be.

The temporal life is like a vessel sailing over eternal waters, a vessel that can be abandoned at any time for the promise of rebirth; to be born anew into a state of eternal consciousness . . . (but this is only the beginning of awakening).

Because one's time and energy are not infinite is it not wise to spend as much of them as possible on what promotes and celebrates manifestation of the infinite?

75

Many busy themselves with nothing but the day-to-day, living with their souls asleep.

Everyone lives in the universe, but the universe does not *live* in all . . . (though could in all).

.

If nothing else should not human life be a
progression of spiritual awakening . . .

What valid excuse exists for not growing
spiritually until one's final breath?

Whatever one learns from a lesson or experience there is always more to be learned from it, providing one continues to reflect upon it.

There is never any other place for one to be than where one is at any given moment, but there may be more for one to do.

Finding peace in one's life has more to do with one's inner state than it does the outer world.

The inner peace of enlightenment is not one of stagnant bliss or self-satisfaction; it is the condition that allows one to move to greater wisdom and acceptance of what must be experienced to achieve it.

What is the peace worth that is void of growth
and creative power?

What interferes with the health and development
of the inner life is toxic to life, for it is there
where all love grows, where all treasure of the
spirit takes root and evolves that can reduce
the poisons of evil and hatred in the world.

To grow spiritually is to engage one's life
in the central duty of the human species.

Note the power of a single atom when
harnessed correctly, and that you are made
of billions of atoms . . . might the spiritual
dimension have a counterpart to the atom?
If so, what power might be released if
harnessed correctly . . .

INTO THE INNER LIFE

Like running on a wheel going round and round
spinning in place, going nowhere . . . this, like
the affairs of the everyday world, really going
nowhere, when there's another realm to explore,
offering freedom, discovery and adventure
beyond anything you see before you can offer
you. All that is needed to begin the experience is
to step off the wheel and begin the inner journey.

In moments throughout the journey there are
echoes of what one was and hints of what one
will become.

How one evolves spiritually takes place
far out of range of everyone's vision.

The more unique the productions of a
human being the more unique the path
that was travelled to realize them.

Every individual in the midst of substantive
growth is confronted with the question if he
or she will pay the price — the price to
be oneself.

It is in the striving, not in the attainment
where one tests oneself, strengthens oneself,
and creates the marrow of one's life that enables
one to go on, to endure, to persevere and
achieve the best that one is capable of
achieving.

84

Scaling Mt. Everest is impressive, but what is
this compared to scaling the Everest of the
soul . . .

To face oneself, confront oneself, demand
of oneself daily to be the best that one can be
is to do a rare and noble thing.

Before one discovers his wisdom he must make the humbling acquaintance of his folly.

Mind, spirit, character do not develop on their own.

One must travel a long way spiritually before seeing how far one needs to go.

The greatest awakenings are achieved in places where there is no support, where there is only room for one.

There is a place in the journey toward the extraordinary where the traveller must leave everything behind, as if saying to a companion that has accompanied one to that point: "From here I must go on alone."

There is only one Holy Grail, but there are other grails . . . as many as there are spirits who have the courage to go in search of the one that is their own.

88

If you embrace the best that is in you the worst the world has to give you can never destroy you.

A bullet can take one's life, but no weapon exists nor will ever exist that can destroy one's truth.

It is all inside you, but the "I" (the ego) needs to be lost to realize this.

Wisdom is impossible in the absence of honesty with oneself.

To see oneself one must first get *beyond* oneself, but all understanding of self comes from ground level (from depth level).

The knowledge that demands the highest price for its attainment is self-knowledge.

To live in the sun rather than the shadow of one's
life requires above all to be true to one's life.

Do your goals harmonize with your path . . .
if not, then you have acquired the wrong
goals, or are on the wrong path.

One must wake to the dance of one's life
or perish to the march of others.

If you cannot find the answers to your life
within yourself, can you really find them
anywhere else . . .

It is in aloneness where one digests one's experiences, where the lessons of what they have to teach are most clearly understood.

There is always something inside you that knows what you need or need to do . . . always.

94

If you are not yourself in everything you say and
do as you move about the world then who are you,
moving about the world . . .

Only one who stands firmly in his or her truth
can defend their life against the falsehoods of
the world.

What fruitless wanderings has man often
engaged in, neglecting his soul for the
foolish demands of the temporal.

Each must make one's own way, must build
one's own bridge to cross over from the temporal
to the eternal.

Without the cultivation of an inner life one could build the greatest empire the world has ever known and still not know fulfillment.

The world has tied strings to you . . . are you ready to untie them — to turn back into yourself — to release yourself into the custody of yourself . . .

97

To embrace your inner power is to discover
a place within you where even death
cannot go.

Do you have the heart for it, the courage
for it, the spirit for it — to dance in the
sacred fire . . .

If all of life were to suddenly go dark would you
shadow your light to join with the darkness . . .

To shed down to one's bare essence is to become
spirit, to become light bringing energy forever
new to the inner life.

Being — shedding down, dissolving into
fullness.

To get to the depths, to the heights, to love,
to wisdom, to truth, ego must be abandoned.

The greatest gifts are those that are meant
to be served.

The larger the ego the smaller its world.

There can be ego without individuality, and individuality without ego.

Life at its richest is a process of growing into living for something that is greater than oneself.

The great passions are the ones that bear fruit that are of benefit to all.

They know the highest degrees of thought and creativity who have freed themselves from the I of themselves.

They grow wings who strive to better themselves; they draw chains who strive to get the better of others.

The spiritually aware know that everything good in their lives is not for them to keep for themselves alone but to pass on, either directly or transformed.

What is one here for if not to love, if not to give, if not to learn, if not to grow?

For a hand to give or receive it needs to be open . . . so too the mind, heart and spirit.

The most suffocating of prisons is that of selfishness.

Divine love lifts one up to all stages of enlightenment, always at the stage that one has prepared oneself to be.

Can a garden flourish if the gardener has not toiled in it? Or be more healthy, more beautiful or fruitful than the work that has been invested in its care? And can the nature of a spiritual garden be different? Be richer, or yield more than the measure of devotion given to its care?

The roses of the spirit also have thorns, but the blood they draw goes to the soil of one's being (spiritual soil) bringing new flowerings into being.

The times when life does one the most spiritual good are the times when it gives one the most trying challenge.

How many blessings have adorned people's lives without having once been thought of as blessings.

With every task life gives you another chance
to deepen yourself — to learn more about
yourself.

Where you are, right now in your life . . . what
lessons are there to learn? What work is to be
done? What is there to be faced, to be ignored,
to be embraced . . .

Every moment life beckons one to come to greater life.

Why fret over anything the world may keep from you when so many riches of the spirit are waiting to receive you, to offer themselves to you . . .

Nothing you seek from the outer world is better
than what you have within you, but you will
have to go to the depths of yourself to reach it.

The spiritual journey and inner journey are one.

One cannot make one's way to the eternal with pride, but with humility; not with self-interest, but selflessness; not with a desire for gain, but a yearning to give.

The final stage of spiritual transcendence is not a surrender to a power outside oneself, but the complete surrender to the power within.

INTO THE INNER LIFE

To surrender is to triumph in the realm of the
spiritual.

We are born in the field of time given a temporal
life, but with that life comes a privilege to connect
with the eternal, a spark inside all that is of the
eternal, but one that must be ignited, to set the
flame, to birth the dawn of awakening that leads
with increasing clarity to the realization that
there is so much more than what we see before
us, to stir the sense of wonder and awe of the
miracle of which we are a part, the power of
that miracle lying always within you.

Beyond all advantages and disadvantages, beyond
all gain and loss — a state of spiritual light
as luminous as
the measure of inner depth that is created . . . this
the
promise
of the inner life.

It truly is all inside you.
Are you on the journey
that will take you to
this discovery

. . . . .

ABOUT THE AUTHOR

Carroll Blair is an author of more than twenty
books and the recipient of numerous awards.
His work has been well endorsed and com-
mendably reviewed. Among his titles cited
for distinction are *Through the Shadows,* winner
of the *Pacific Book Awards*, and *Quarter Notes*,
winner of the *Sharp Writ Book Awards.*
He is an alumnus of the Boston Conservatory
and lives in Massachusetts.